KIDS IN HISTORY

How Did Kids Live in the American Colonies?

BY MEGAN QUICK

Gareth Stevens PUBLISHING

Please visit our website, www.garethstevens.com. For a free color catalog of all our high-quality books, call toll free 1-800-542-2595 or fax 1-877-542-2596.

Cataloging-in-Publication Data

Names: Quick, Megan.
Title: How did kids live in the American colonies? / Megan Quick.
Description: New York : Gareth Stevens Publishing, 2024. | Series: Kids in history | Includes glossary and index.
Identifiers: ISBN 9781538288214 (pbk.) | ISBN 9781538288221 (library bound) | ISBN 9781538288238 (ebook)
Subjects: LCSH: Children–United States–History–17th century–Juvenile literature. | Children–United States–History–18th century–Juvenile literature. | United States–Social life and customs–To 1775–Juvenile literature. | United States–History–Colonial period, ca. 1600-1775–Juvenile literature.
Classification: LCC E188.Q75 2024 | DDC 973.2–dc23

Portions of this work were originally authored by Sarah Machajewski and published as *A Kid's Life in Colonial America*. All new material in this edition was authored by Megan Quick.

Published in 2024 by
Gareth Stevens Publishing
2544 Clinton Street
Buffalo, NY 14224

Designer: Jen Schoembs
Editor: Megan Quick

Photo credits: Cover, p. 1 (house) Bob Didner/iStock.com; cover, p. 1 (girl) Gelpi/Shutterstock.com; cover (background), p.1 (background), series art (background) Login/Shutterstock.com; p. 5 Anadolu_Dizgi/Shutterstock.com; p. 7 Unknown Author/BattleOfBloodyBrook.jpg/commons.wikimedia.org; p. 9 H. J. Rhodes/Wallach Division Picture Collection/New York Public Library; p. 10 David Ross/Shutterstock.com; p. 11 Benjamin Franklin Collection/Library of Congress; p. 13 Jean-François Millet/Woman Churning Butter/commons.wikimedia.org; p. 14 Walpot, H./Abc-boekje met gotische letters/commons.wikimedia.org; p. 15 North Wind Picture Archives/Alamy.com; p. 17 ZU_09/iStock.com; p. 19 netop2all/iStock.com; p. 21 John Trumbull/The Declaration of Independence/commons.wikimedia.org.

Printed in the United States of America

CPSIA compliance information: Batch #CS24GS: For further information contact Gareth Stevens at 1-800-542-2595.

Contents

Coming to America 4
Not the First 6
Home Life 8
Colonial Fashion 10
Feeding the Family 12
Education in the Colonies 14
Going to Church 16
Child's Play 18
A New Beginning 20
Glossary 22
For More Information 23
Index 24

Words in the glossary appear in **bold** type the first time they are used in the text.

Coming to America

In the early 1600s, thousands of Europeans traveled to North America to start a new life. When they arrived, they set up farms and towns. They built houses, churches, and schools. Over the next 100 years, the settlers created 13 **colonies.**

There was lots of work to do in colonial America. Even children worked hard. Kids helped with farming, made clothes, and cared for babies. There was little time for playing, or even school. Let's learn more about the American colonies and what life was like for kids.

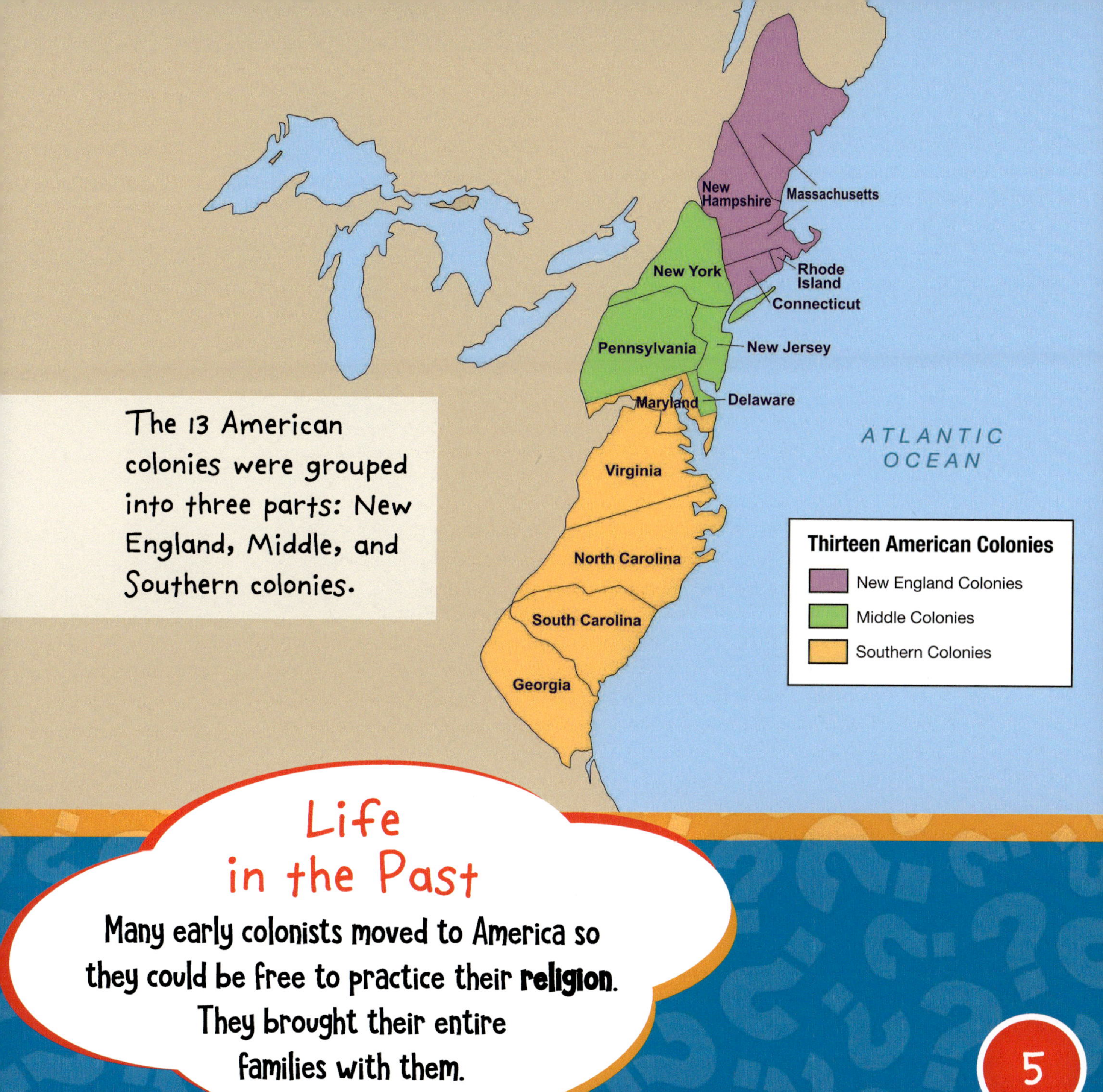

The 13 American colonies were grouped into three parts: New England, Middle, and Southern colonies.

Life in the Past

Many early colonists moved to America so they could be free to practice their **religion**. They brought their entire families with them.

Not the First

The European colonists weren't the first people to make their home in what is now the United States. American Indians had been living in North and South America for thousands of years. Sometimes the colonists and **Indigenous** people were able to work together. But often the groups **clashed.**

The colonists took over the American Indians' land. They brought sicknesses that were deadly to the Indigenous people. Some colonists **enslaved** American Indians as well as Black people. The American Indians fought back, but it became harder to fight as more Europeans arrived.

There were many fights between colonists and American Indians, such as the Battle of Bloody Brook in 1675, shown here.

Home Life

When the colonists arrived in America, it was mostly **wilderness.** They chopped down the trees to make wood houses, shops, and churches. Often parents, aunts, uncles, and cousins lived together in one house.

Running the home was hard work. Most things were done by hand, and everyone had jobs. Men and boys cared for animals, planted crops, chopped wood, and fixed tools. Women and girls made clothes, butter, soap, and candles for the family. Sometimes girls helped with outdoor chores as well.

Life in the Past

Children learned how to work at a very young age. Often, a girl as young as 4 years old knew how to **knit** socks.

A girl brings in the cows from the fields at the end of the day.

Colonial Fashion

In the early years, most people in the colonies made their own clothes. Girls learned how to spin thread to make cloth. Their mothers showed them how to make wool and **linen.** They used berries, tree bark, and walnut shells to dye the clothing.

spinning wheel

Colonial children often dressed in the same style as the adults. Women and girls wore long dresses with **petticoats** underneath. They wore leather shoes and caps. Men and boys wore **breeches,** long shirts, and leather shoes.

Life in the Past

Winters in the colonies could be very cold. Girls stayed warm in hooded **cloaks,** while boys wore leather breeches, wool shirts, and boots.

Most clothing in the colonies was simple and **practical.** Children might have one good outfit for church on Sunday.

Feeding the Family

Colonial children played an important role in growing and preparing food. Families grew most of their food themselves. The colonists learned about growing food from the American Indians. They taught the colonists how to grow and care for the crops that grew best on American land.

Children helped their parents plant and gather grains, fruits, and vegetables. Families raised cows, pigs, and chickens for food. Boys and girls helped care for the animals. They also fished. Food was cooked over the fireplace.

A young girl helps her family by churning butter.

Life in the Past

Children were often in charge of making butter. They separated cream from cow's milk and then turned the cream to butter by mixing it in a tool called a butter churn.

Education in the Colonies

When the settlers first arrived in America, there were no schools as we've come to know them. Children learned their ABCs at home. As time went on, the colonists built one-room schoolhouses. Students of all ages were in the same classroom together. The youngest students sat in the front. The oldest sat in the back.

hornbook

Many teachers didn't have much training. The students said lessons over and over until they knew them by memory. They used hornbooks for their lessons. These were boards that had the alphabet, numbers, and prayers on them.

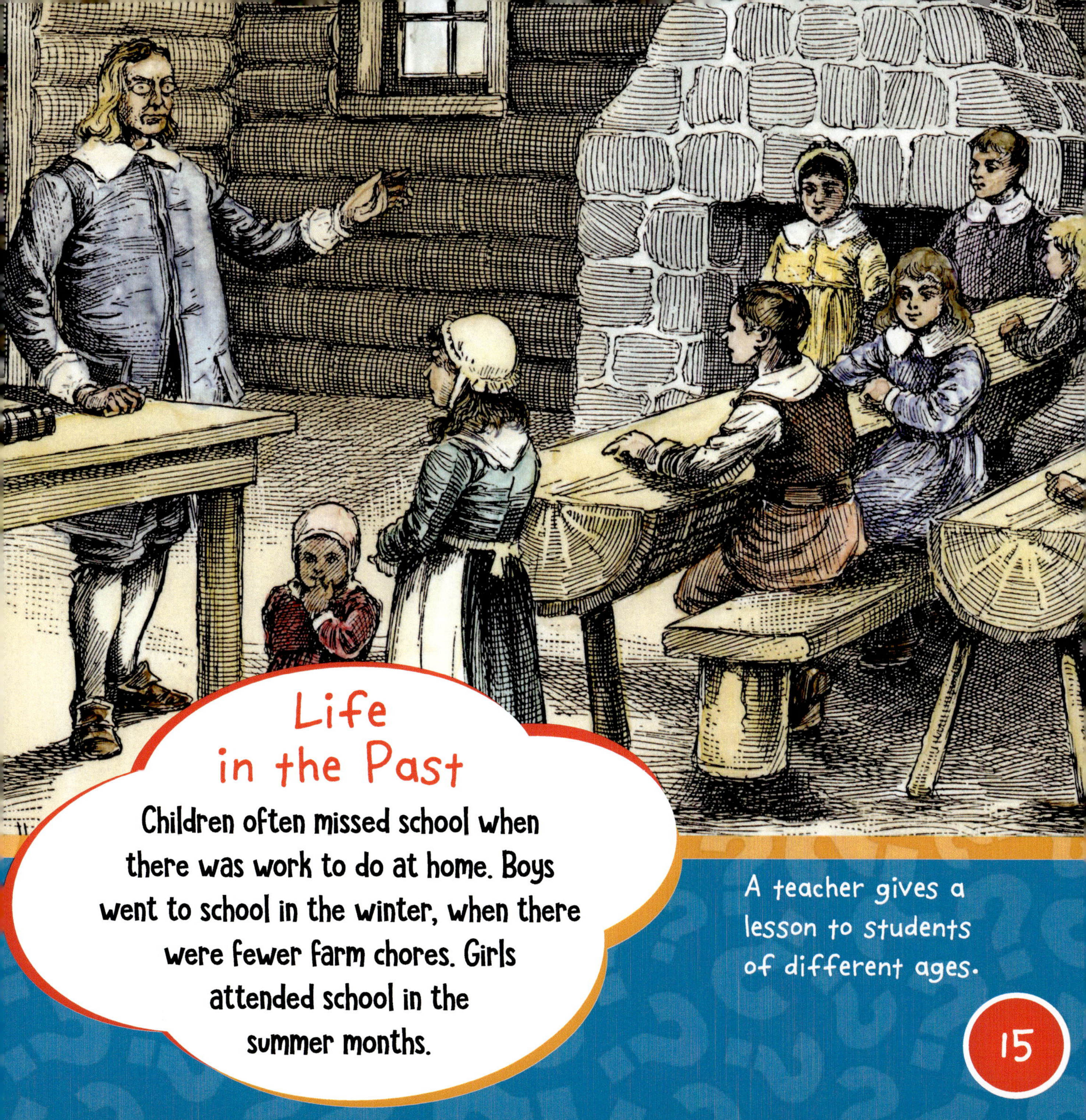

Life in the Past

Children often missed school when there was work to do at home. Boys went to school in the winter, when there were fewer farm chores. Girls attended school in the summer months.

A teacher gives a lesson to students of different ages.

Going to Church

Colonists worked hard all week, but Sunday was a day to rest. Most people went to church. In fact, in areas such as New England and Virginia, skipping church was against the law. Church leaders also made rules about how people should dress, act, and speak.

Children went with their families to church. It often lasted for many hours—sometimes all day. Kids had to sit quietly on hard wooden benches. They could get in a lot of trouble for not paying attention.

Life in the Past

In New England, boys often had to sit up front in church. This allowed the church leaders to keep an eye on them.

Here, colonists attend church in Plymouth, Massachusetts, in the 1620s.

Child's Play

Kids in colonial America liked to have fun. When their chores were done, they found plenty of ways to enjoy themselves. Children went swimming and fishing in the summer and sledding in the winter. They played hopscotch, tag, and hide-and-seek.

Toys were much simpler in colonial times. Girls played with dolls made from rags or leftover pieces of cloth. They built their own kites and shot marbles. Another popular activity was racing each other while rolling a large hoop.

A little boy rolls a hoop like the ones colonial children used.

A New Beginning

England ruled the American colonies. Each colony had its own government, but the British were still in charge. Over the years, the colonists became more and more unhappy with British rule. The two sides went to war. After more than eight years of fighting, America became free from England.

From the early 1600s to the late 1700s, America changed from mostly wilderness to a busy new nation. American children played a part in helping their families, and their new home, survive and grow.

Life in the Past

The American Revolution began on April 19, 1775, with the Battles of Lexington and Concord. The war ended on September 3, 1783.

Here, the **Founding Fathers** present the Declaration of Independence. When it was approved, the colonies became the United States of America.

Glossary

breeches: Short trousers fitting snugly at or just below the knee.

clash: To come into conflict.

cloak: A long, loose outer garment.

colony: A piece of land under the control of another country.

enslave: Having to do with being owned by another person and forced to work without pay.

Founding Father: A leading figure in the establishment of the United States.

Indigenous: The earliest known people living in an area.

knit: To form a fabric or garment by interlacing yarn or thread in connected loops with needles.

linen: Smooth, strong cloth or yarn made from flax.

petticoat: A slip worn under a skirt or dress.

practical: Useful.

religion: A belief in and way of honoring a god or gods.

wilderness: A piece of uninhabited land left to grow wild.

For More Information

Books

Freeburg, Jessica. *A Jamestown Colony Time Capsule: Artifacts of the Early American Colony.* North Mankato, MN: Capstone Press, 2021.

Greendeer, Danielle, Anthony Perry, and Alexis Bunten. *Keepunumuk: Weeâchumun's Thanksgiving Story.* Watertown, MA: Charlesbridge, 2022.

O'Neill, Sean. *50 Things You Didn't Know About Colonial America.* South Egremont, MA: Red Chair Press, 2020.

Websites

Ducksters: Colonial America for Kids
www.ducksters.com/history/colonial_america/
Take a closer look at the people, places, events, and daily life of colonial America.

National Park Service
www.nps.gov/articles/000/colonial-games.htm
Check out some toys and games used in colonial times, and then create your own toy.

PBS: Liberty! Daily Life in the Colonies
www.pbs.org/ktca/liberty/perspectives_daily.html
Click on the pictures to find out about colonial life in New England.

Publisher's note to educators and parents: Our editors have carefully reviewed these websites to ensure that they are suitable for students. Many websites change frequently, however, and we cannot guarantee that a site's future contents will continue to meet our high standards of quality and educational value. Be advised that students should be closely supervised whenever they access the internet.

Index

American Indians, 6, 7, 12
American Revolution, 20, 21
Battle of Bloody Brook, 7
Battles of Lexington and Concord, 21
childcare, 4
chores, 8, 9, 12, 13, 15, 18
clothing/sewing, 4, 8, 9, 10, 11, 16
Declaration of Independence, 21
education, 4, 14, 15
enslavement, 6
family, 5, 8
farming, 4, 8, 12, 15
food/cooking, 8, 12, 13
Founding Fathers, 21
home, 4, 8
illness, 6
livestock, 8, 9, 12
play, 4, 18, 19
religion, 4, 5, 16
war, 20, 21